KRYPTO
The SUPERDOG

SUPERMAN CREATED BY
JERRY SIEGEL AND JOE SHUSTER
BY SPECIAL ARRANGEMENT WITH
THE JERRY SIEGEL FAMILY

Raintree

Raintree is an imprint of Capstone Global
Library Limited, a company incorporated
in England and Wales having its registered
office at 7 Pilgrim Street, London, EC4V
6LB - Registered company number: 6695582

First published by Raintree in 2014
The moral rights of the proprietor have
been asserted.

Originally published by DC Comics in the
US in single magazine form as Krypto The
Superdog #2.

Ashley C. Andersen Zantop Publisher
Michael Dahl Editorial Director
Donald Lemke & Sean Tulien Editors
Bob Lentz Art Director
Hilary Wacholz Designer

DC COMICS
Kristy Quinn Original US Editor

ISBN 978 1 406 27951 1

Printed in China by Nordica.
0314/CA21400432
17 16 15 14
10 9 8 7 6 5 4 3 2 1

British Library Cataloguing in Publication
Data
A full catalogue record for this book is
available from the British Library.

KRYPTO

The SUPERDOG ™

Crisis of Infinite Kryptos

JESSE LEON MCCANN.................................WRITER

MIN S. KU ....PENCILLER

JEFF ALBRECHT .... INKER

DAVE TANGUAY ....COLOURIST

DAVE TANGUAY ....LETTERER

CRISIS
OF INFINITE KRYPTOS

JESSE LEON MCCANN · WRITER
MIN S. KU · PENCILLER
JEFF ALBRECHT · INKER
DAVE TANGUAY · LETTERER/COLORIST
RACHEL GLUCKSTERN · ASST. EDITOR
JOAN HILTY · EDITOR

WAIT THERE. I'M GOING FOR *A QUICK SPIN!*

FWOOSH!

WHRRRRR!

BECAUSE THIS LOOKS LIKE A JOB FOR *SUPERDOG!*

BA-THOOM!

RUFF, RUFF AND *AWAY!*

AWESOME!

ZZZIP!

WOW! I WONDER WHERE THIS *BAD BOY* CAME FROM?

SIZZLE!

CRACK!

W-WAIT! WHAT IF THERE'S SOME KIND OF *BLOB-THING* IN THERE, JUST WAITING TO *EAT US?*

I *DOUBT* THAT. STILL, WE'D BETTER *BE CAREFUL.*

CRACK!

HISSSSSS!

OH, NO! *RED KRYPTONITE!*

REMEMBER? IT HAS *WEIRD, UNPREDICTABLE EFFECTS* ON ANYONE FROM *KRYPTON,* LIKE *SUPERMAN...OR ME!*

KA-THUNK!

EWOO-EWOO-EWOO!

EEEEEEK! ANIMALS! ANIMALS ARE IN OUR CITY!

YAAAAAH! EVERYBODY PANIC AND RUN!

THEY'LL CHEW OUR ROOTS AND DIG UP THE ELDERLY! HELP! POLICE!

I DON'T EVEN LIKE TO CHEW ON ROOTS. MAYBE WE SHOULD JUST LEAVE QUIETLY.

THIS IS WEIRD! WE DIDN'T DO ANYTHING.

OUT TO LUNCH

YOU'RE NOT GOING ANYWHERE! YOU'VE BROKEN THE LAW!

WHAT? WHO...?

I'M SUPERDOG, AND THIS IS YOUR UNLUCKY DAY!

BUT, YOU'RE NOT... I MEAN, UH, HE'S ALSO...

WHAT KEVIN'S TRYING TO SAY IS, WE CAME HERE BY AN INTERDIMENSIONAL PORTAL...

IT DOESN'T MATTER HOW YOU GOT HERE, IT'S AGAINST THE LAW FOR ANIMALS OF ANY KIND TO ENTER TREEOPOLIS.

SORRY, GUYS, IT'S A VERY SERIOUS CRIME. YOU SHOULDN'T HAVE IGNORED THE SIGNS AND FENCES!

LOOK, WE DIDN'T MEAN TO CAUSE ANY TROUBLE. WE'LL JUST BE ON OUR WAY.

HEY, COME BACK HERE! IT'S NOT THAT EASY!

WHOOSH

YOU'RE GOING TO JAIL!

WHAM!

WHOA!

UGH! CUT IT OUT!

HEY! WHY ARE YOU IN *LINES* LIKE THIS?

DON'T YOU *REMEMBER*? WE WERE *CLONED* BY *WIZARD SNOOKY* SO WE COULD SERVE *LORD MECHANIKAT* NIGHT AND DAY.

THOSE *PHONIES*? WHY DON'T YOU *FIGHT BACK*?

ARE YOU *CRAZY*, KID? MECHANIKAT WOULD *DESTROY* US ALL!

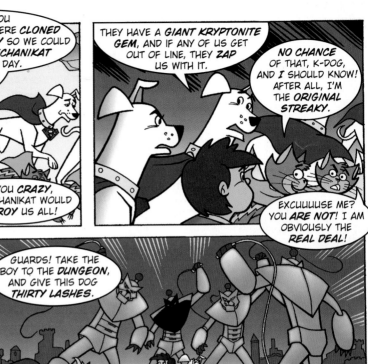

THEY HAVE A *GIANT KRYPTONITE GEM*, AND IF ANY OF US GET OUT OF LINE, THEY *ZAP* US WITH IT.

NO CHANCE OF THAT, K-DOG, AND *I* SHOULD KNOW! AFTER ALL, I'M THE *ORIGINAL STREAKY*.

EXCUUUUSE ME? YOU *ARE NOT*! I AM OBVIOUSLY THE *REAL DEAL*!

WHAT IN THE NAME OF *GALACTIC DOMINATION* IS GOING ON HERE?

GUARDS! TAKE THE BOY TO THE *DUNGEON*, AND GIVE THIS DOG *THIRTY LASHES*.

I DON'T *THINK* SO.

YOUR REIGN OF TERROR IS *OVER*, MECHANIKAT!

AND FOR STARTERS, YOUR CATBOTS ARE IN A *WHIRL* OF *TROUBLE*!

WWHHHRRRRRL

YOU DARE? WIZARD SNOOKY, CALL FORTH THE *ROYAL GEM*!

FLING!

WITH *PLEASURE*, YOUR SUPEREGO-NESS!

MWAH-HAH-HAH-HAH! WHAT DO YOU SAY *NOW*, SMARTY-PANTS?

EWOO-EWOO-EWOO!

BIM-SALLA-BIM, WITH MY MAGIC WAND, I MUSTER THE ROYAL GEM, AND YOU'RE GONNA GET IT, BUSTER!

GAH! I REALLY *HATE* THIS!

OH... SO *WEAK*...

OH, NOW YOU'VE *DONE IT*!

11

I SAY IT'S *TOO BAD* FOR YOU THAT *BLUE KRYPTONITE* DOESN'T AFFECT ME!

RRRRRRRRRRRRRRRRRRR!

KA-BLAM!

WHAT?

SNOOKY! YOU AND I ARE GOING TO *DISCUSS* WHAT WENT WRONG HERE IN *PAINFUL* DETAIL!

GULP! YES, YOUR *BILIOUS-NESS.*

YOU *DID IT,* K-DOG, WE'RE *FREE!* TIME TO *PARTAY-DOWN* IN THE CASTLE!

YAY! HOORAY! CHEER!

ZZZZZUMMMM!

SORRY, STREAKY, WE'VE *GOT TO GO.* BUT I'LL LEAVE IT TO YOU AND THE OTHER *SUPER-PETS* TO *PROTECT* THIS DIMENSION!

HEY, MAYBE WE'RE *BACK HOME.* EVERYTHING LOOKS PRETTY *NORMAL.*

ZZZZZUMMMM!

AFRAID NOT, KEVIN. *LOOK!*

YIKES!

...SINCE WE'RE ONLY TWO INCHES TALL!

Cola-Pop

RETREAT! I REPEAT, *ALL* INVASION TEAMS RETREAT FROM PLANET EARTH!

OH...I GUESS NOT.

MAYBE WE SHOULD *HELP SUPERDOG...* ER, YOURSELF... AH...*HIM?*

SIGH. NO, I DON'T THINK WE'D BE *MUCH HELP* TO HIM...

HA HA HA HA! THE *RUSE* WORKED! ALL OF EARTH'S HEROES ARE *DISTRACTED* BY THE FLEET'S RETREAT, WHILE WE ARE FREE TO *EXACT OUR REVENGE!*

HEH.

HEY, *LOOK.*

SHHH.

BWAH-HAH! SOON THIS **DEVICE** WILL CREATE A **ZDARSIONIC-BURST** THAT WILL BE **AMPLIFIED** BY THE **STEEL STRUCTURE** OF THIS SKYSCRAPER!

AND WHAT **BETTER** PLACE TO SET OFF THE DEVICE THAN METROPOLIS'S VERY OWN **DAILY PLANET** BUILDING?! HA HA HA HA HA!

HEH

FOOLISH EARTHLINGS! THE **AMPLIFIED BURST** WILL **DESTROY EVERY ELECTRONIC DEVICE** ON THE PLANET! NO MORE TELEPHONES, PLANES, AUTOMOBILES, TELEVISIONS OR COMPUTERS... NO MORE CDS, DVDS, MPEGS OR MP3S... NO MORE **AVRIL!**

KEVIN, I THINK IT'S TIME WE **SWAT** SOME BUGS!

YOU **SAID IT!** HEY, ALIENS—THIS IS A **RAID!**

HEH.

WELL, WELL! FOR **LITTLE NUISANCES**, YOU'RE SURE A PAIR OF **BIG BLOWHARDS!**

COME ON, LACKEYS— LET'S SHOW THEM WE CAN BE EVEN **BIGGER** BLOWHARDS...WITH A **VENGEANCE!** HA HA HA HA HA!

WHIRRRRRRRRR!

SLAM! WI

FLAP FLAP FLAP FLAP

WHOOSH!

WHOOOOSH!

UGH!

WHIR

SUPERDOG! ARE YOU **OKAY**, BOY?

I-I **THINK** SO, BUT IT FEELS LIKE SOMETHING IS **SAPPING** MY **ENERGY**...

...BUT NEVER MIND! WE'VE GOT TO **DESTROY** THAT DEVICE!

TIME FOR A LITTLE *SUPER-SPEED*! I HOPE YOU BOYS DON'T HAVE ANY *PLANS* FOR THIS AFTERNOON—BECAUSE YOU'RE GOING TO BE A LITTLE *TIED UP*!

AURGH! IT DOESN'T MATTER, *SUPER-MUTT!* YOU *WON'T* BE ABLE TO *DISABLE* MY DEVICE! THE *KEY* IS MADE OF *GREEN KRYPTONITE!*

THAT'S WHAT WAS *SAPPING MY STRENGTH*— KRYPTONITE! KEVIN, I *CAN'T STOP* THE BURST!

BUT *I CAN!*

NOOOO!

OUTSIDE...

HEY! WHAT'S GOING *ON* HERE?

THERE! THIS *AREA* IS NOW OFFICIALLY A *NO-PEST STRIP!*

YOU BOYS DOING SOME OF *MY WORK* FOR ME? WHO ARE YOU?

OH, HI! THIS IS KEVIN, AND *I'M... YOU.*

LISTEN, IT'S A *LONG STORY*, AND WE'VE GOT A *PORTAL* TO CATCH. JUST REMEMBER US AS YOUR *LITTLE HELPERS!*

COOL!

ZZZZZZUMMMM!

SEVERAL DOZEN ADVENTURES LATER...

WHEW! I THOUGHT WE'D *NEVER* SEE *OUR DIMENSION* AGAIN!

ZZZZZZUMMMM!

WE BETTER FLY BACK TO OUR HOUSE, JUST AS SOON AS I *TOSS* THIS RED KRYPTONITE WHERE IT'LL NEVER *BOTHER* US AGAIN!

GOOD! THE *UNIVERSE* IS A *NICE PLACE* TO VISIT, BUT THERE'S *NO PLACE* LIKE HOME!

THE **END**

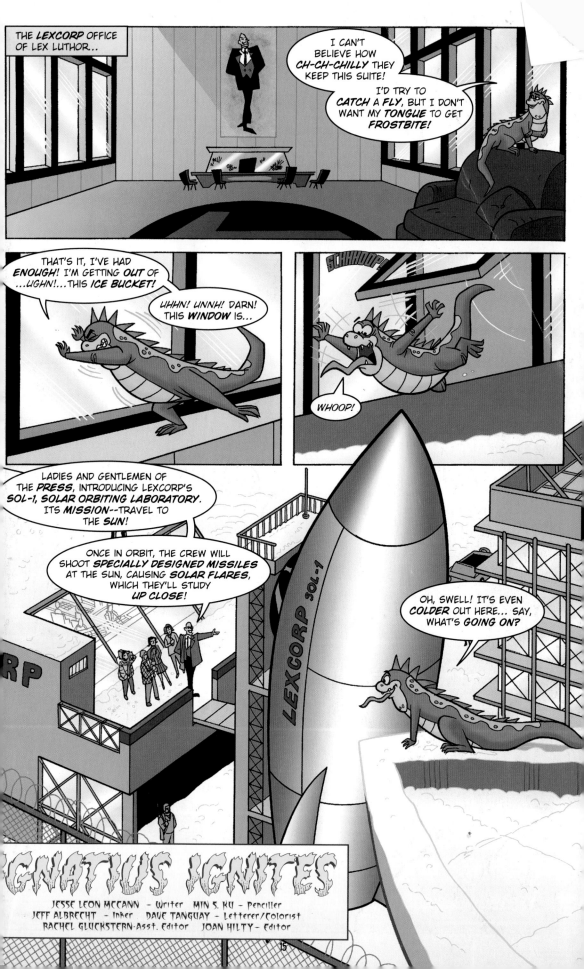

BUT, *MR. LUTHOR*, WON'T YOUR ROCKET SHIP *MELT*?

IT WILL GET VERY *HOT INSIDE*, MISS LANE. BUT THE SHIP AND CREW WILL *SURVIVE*, THANKS TO THE *ULTRA-REFRIGERATION SYSTEM* I'VE DEVISED.

VERY *HOT INSIDE*?! OH, JOY! BLISS! I HAVE *GOT* TO *STOW AWAY* ON THAT SHIP!

A SHORT WHILE LATER...

ON THE OTHER HAND, *WHY WAIT*? BON VOYAGE, *POPSICLES*! I'M GOING TO WHERE IT'S *WARM* AND *SUNNY* ALL THE TIME!

RRRRROAR!

TZZZOOOOM!

OPERATING THIS SHIP IS *EASY*! THANKS TO THE *INSTRUCTION MANUAL*, A LI'L *LIZARD'S EGG* COULD DO IT!

DAYS LATER, IN ORBIT AROUND THE SUN...

NICE, BUT I WANT IT *HOTTER*!

I'LL *FIRE A MISSILE*. A SOLAR FLARE SHOULD *WARM* THINGS UP!

110° TEMP

FWHOOSH!

WELL, *BAKE* MY *HOT CROSS BUNS*, IT WORKED! *WOOT! WOOT!*

GEE! I *WONDER* WHAT WOULD HAPPEN IF I FIRED A *DOZEN MISSILES* AT ONCE?

120° TEMP

SIZZLE! CRACKLE!

LATER, BACK ON *EARTH*...

I GUESS IT'S NICE THEY GET TO *ENJOY* THE *POOL* SO MUCH.

BUT THEY *SHOULDN'T* BE ABLE TO AT 6:30 AM!

AND THEY *ABSOLUTELY SHOULDN'T* BE ABLE TO IN *NOVEMBER*!

NOVEMBER

HOT, KEVIN! *TOO HOT!*

YOU SAID IT, MELANIE! THIS *HEAT WAVE'S* BEEN GOING ON *TOO* LONG!

LUCKY FOR ME, *SUPERMAN ELEMENTARY* HAS AWESOME *AIR CONDITIONING!*

SOMETHING'S AFFECTING *EARTH'S WEATHER*, BUT WHAT? MAYBE THE *DOG STAR PATROL* CAN HELP.

C'MON, STREAKY!

AW, CAN'T I JUST CURL UP *INSIDE* THE *FREEZER* AND TAKE A *NAP?*

KRYPTO

YES, SUPERDOG, *SENSORS* ARE PICKING UP AN *UNKNOWN ANOMALY* NEAR *SOL*, WHAT YOU *EARTHLINGS* CALL "THE SUN."

WE'LL SWING BY *EARTH* TO PICK YOU UP!

GREAT! TO COOL THINGS DOWN, WE'RE GOING TO THE *HOTTEST PLACE* IN THE SOLAR SYSTEM!

THE *DOG STAR PATROL* SHIP...

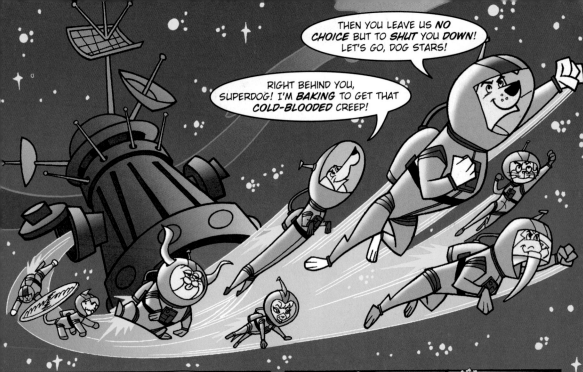

AND A *QUICK STOP* TO GET YOU *WHIRLING PESTS* OUT OF MY WAY!

WAAAAH!

FLING!

FLING!

HEY, WATCH IT! *HOT STUFF* FLOATIN' HERE!

EXCORP 300-8

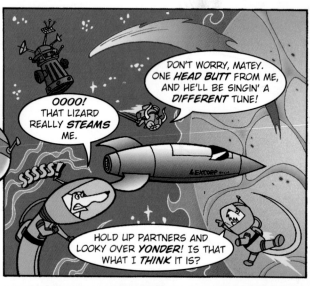

OOOO! THAT LIZARD REALLY *STEAMS* ME.

DON'T WORRY, MATEY. ONE *HEAD BUTT* FROM ME, AND HE'LL BE SINGIN' A *DIFFERENT* TUNE!

SSSSS!

HOLD UP PARTNERS AND LOOKY OVER *YONDER*! IS THAT WHAT I *THINK* IT IS?

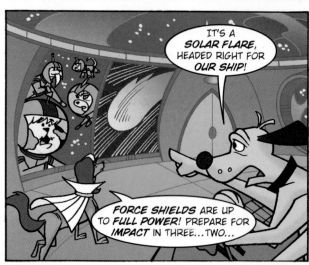

IT'S A *SOLAR FLARE*, HEADED RIGHT FOR *OUR SHIP!*

FORCE SHIELDS ARE UP TO *FULL POWER*! PREPARE FOR *IMPACT* IN THREE...TWO...

THE SHIELDS ARE *PROTECTING* US!

CRACKLE!

WHOOOSH!

GOOD SHOW, GOV-NAH MA'AM!

BUT OUR *POWER LEVELS* ARE DOWN.

HOPEFULLY, PAW POOCH CAN *REPLACE* OUR *FRIED CIRCUIT BOARDS* BEFORE IGNATIUS FIRES *ANOTHER ROCKET!*

POWERLEV

HELLOOOOO? I *ALREADY FIRED* ANOTHER ROCKET!

WELL, *WHAT* ARE YOU WAITING FOR? DON'T YOU THINK YOU SHOULD TRY TO GET YOUR *CRIPPLED SHIP* OUT OF HERE BEFORE IT'S *TOO LATE?*

HEY, K-DOG, MAYBE WE SHOULD TRY *PUSHING* THE DOG STAR PATROL'S SHIP OUT OF *HARM'S WAY?*

IF SOMETHING *HAPPENS* TO IT, WE'LL BE *DOG-PADDLING* HOME!

JUST GIVE THINGS A *FEW MORE* SECONDS.

IGNATIUS, HAVEN'T YOU *NOTICED* THAT IT'S GETTING A *LITTLE TOO HOT* IN THERE?

NOW THAT YOU *MENTION* IT, I WAS STARTING TO *SWEAT A TEENSY BIT.*

BUT *NO MATTER!* I'LL JUST *TURN UP* THE *REFRIGERATION...* GREAT 'GATOR ON A GO-CART! THE *SWITCH* IS *BROKEN!*

IF YOU CAUSE ANY MORE *SOLAR FLARES,* IT'LL GET EVEN *HOTTER.*

HOW CAN THIS *BE?* IT *MUST* BE SOME SORT OF *TRICK!*

I'D BETTER *MAKE SURE* THE SHIP IS REALLY *HEATING UP.*

IGNATIUS, I'D SAY YOU JUST GOT A *HOT TIP!*

SSSSS!

YEOWCH!

IF YOU PROMISE TO *TURN AROUND* AND GO HOME *RIGHT NOW,* BRAINY CAN TURN YOUR *REFRIGERATION* BACK ON WITH HER *TELEPATHY.*

NOW YOU KNOW HOW THE *PEOPLE OF EARTH* FEEL!

SO HOT... THIRSTY...

ESSSSSS!

Superdog Jokes!

WHAT DID THE TIRED DOG SAY?

I'VE HAD A RUFF DAY!

WHAT DID THE DOG CATCHER SAY TO HIS DENTIST?

I HAVE A FEW LOOSE CANINES!

WHAT KIND OF DOG DOES DRACULA HAVE?

A BLOODHOUND!

WHAT DID THE DOGGY CARPENTER SPECIALIZE IN?

ROOFING!

JESSE LEON MCCANN WRITER

Jesse Leon McCann is a *New York Times* Top-Ten Children's Book Writer, as well as a prolific all-ages comics writer. His credits include Pinky and the Brain, Animaniacs, and Looney Tunes for DC Comics; Scooby-Doo and Shrek 2 for Scholastic; and The Simpsons and Futurama for Bongo Comics. He lives in Los Angeles with his wife and four cats.

MIN SUNG KU PENCILLER

As a young child, Min Sung Ku dreamt of becoming a comic book illustrator. At six years old, he drew a picture of Superman standing behind the American flag. He has since achieved his childhood dream, having illustrated popular licensed comics properties such as the Justice League, Batman Beyond, Spider-Man, Ben 10, Phineas & Ferb, the Replacements, the Proud Family, Krypto the Superdog, and, of course, Superman. Min lives with his lovely wife and their beautiful twin daughters, Elisia and Eliana.

DAVE TANGUAY COLOURIST/LETTERER

David Tanguay has over 20 years of experience in the comic book industry. He has worked as an editor, layout artist, colourist, and letterer. He has also done web design, and he taught computer graphics at the State University of New York.

AMPLIFY make something louder or stronger

BRANCH part of a tree that grows out from the trunk, or a specific part of an organization

DIMENSION another space and time

DOMINATION total control

MELLOW soft or calm

METEOR piece of rock or metal from space that enters Earth's atmosphere at high speed, burns, and forms a streak of light as it falls to Earth

NUISANCE thing or person that annoys and causes problems

PANIC struck with sudden terror or fear

SUITE connected series of rooms to be used together, such as a hotel suite

Visual Questions & Prompts

1. THE WORD "BRANCH" IN THIS PANEL HAS TWO MEANINGS. CAN YOU EXPLAIN BOTH OF THEM?

SUPERDOG, *HELP!*

KEVIN!

DON'T WORRY, A *SPECIAL BRANCH* OF OUR *POLICE* WILL CATCH HIM.

1

2. WHY DOES THE BACKGROUND IMAGE OF THIS PANEL HAVE SO MANY DIFFERENT IMAGES? EXPLAIN.

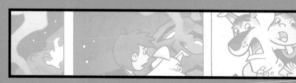

2

3. WHY DO YOU THINK THE ILLUSTRATOR ADDED LINES IN THE BACKGROUND OF THIS PANEL?

GASP!

3

4. WHICH MEMBER OF THE DOG STAR PATROL IS YOUR FAVOURITE? WHY? [SEE PAGE 18 FOR DETAILS.]

4

HIGH-TEMP SUITS